PETER KENT

Hidden Under the Sea

The World Beneath the Waves

DUTTON CHILDREN'S BOOKS ◆ NEW YORK

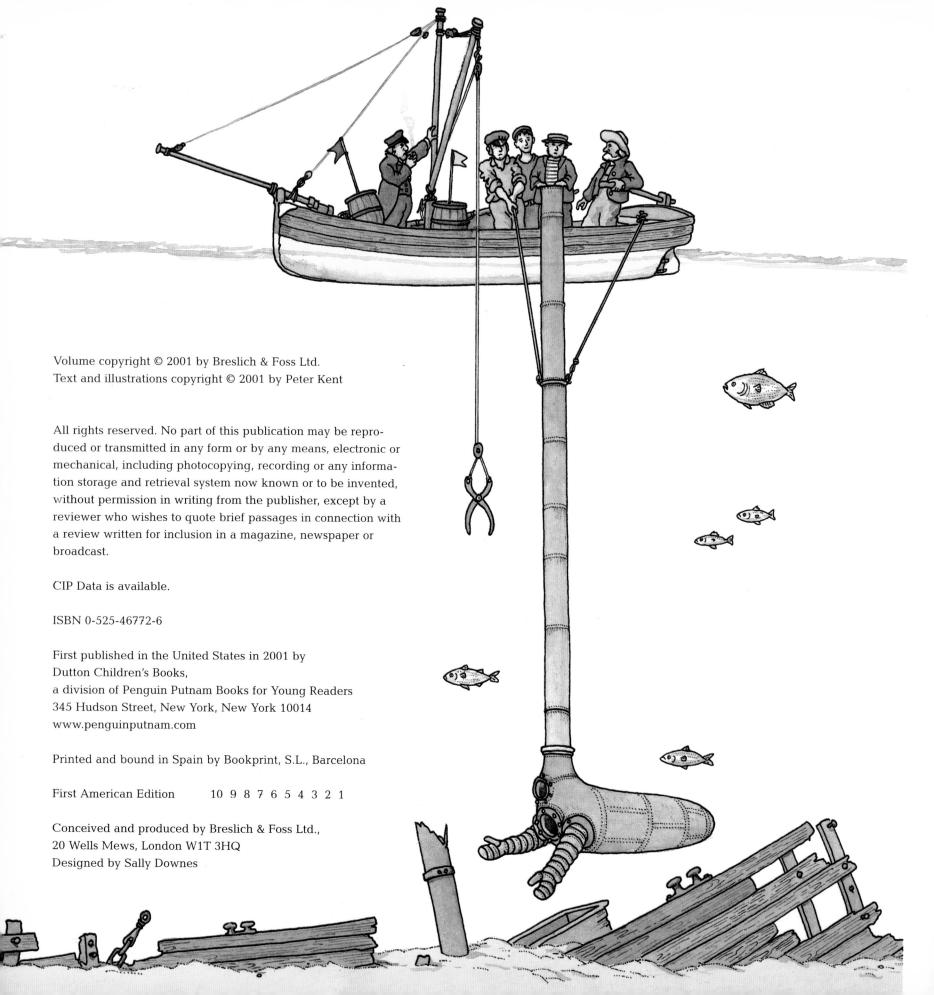

Volume copyright © 2001 by Breslich & Foss Ltd.

Text and illustrations copyright © 2001 by Peter Kent

CIP Data is available.

ISBN 0-525-46772-6

First published in the United States in 2001 by
Dutton Children's Books,
a division of Penguin Putnam Books for Young Readers
345 Hudson Street, New York, New York 10014
www.penguinputnam.com

Printed and bound in Spain by Bookprint, S.L., Barcelona

First American Edition   10 9 8 7 6 5 4 3 2 1

Conceived and produced by Breslich & Foss Ltd.,
20 Wells Mews, London W1T 3HQ
Designed by Sally Downes

CONTENTS

DIVING UNDERWATER

The sea is a mysterious, watery other world that covers almost 75 percent of the earth's surface. The deepest point is the Marianas Trench in the Pacific Ocean, where the seabed plunges down to 36,200 ft. (11,034 m); that's a mile (1.6 km) deeper than Mount Everest is high! The average depth is 13,100 ft. (4,000 m), and below about 3,000 ft. (900 m) there is no light at all.

 In the ocean depths live millions of creatures that range in size from the largest on the planet—the blue whale, which can grow up to 100 ft. (30 m) in length—to microscopic shrimps called copepods. The first land animals crawled out from the sea millions of years ago, and for thousands of years legends abounded concerning curious creatures of the deep. Although people dreamed of being able to live underwater, it remained a dream. Men and women dived for pearls and seafood, but no one could hold his breath for longer than a couple of minutes.

 The invention of the diving bell allowed people to stay underwater for about twenty minutes. Later, devices such as the diving suit and the submarine enabled people to move and work below the waves. The underwater world was gradually opened up, and sunken ships could be reached and treasure salvaged.

When the Aqua-Lung was invented, divers were freed from clumsy air hoses, and people came closer to their ambition of swimming like fishes. Today thousands of vacationers go scuba diving and enjoy the wonders of the sea. Men and women work and live on the sea bottom, and exploration continues as scientists discover strange creatures and geological marvels such as volcanoes that spout red-hot lava deep beneath the ocean surface.

The most dangerous creatures of the deep are not monstrous squid or gigantic whales, but the submarines that may lurk silently in the depths, each capable of devastating entire continents with the nuclear missiles that it carries.

SUBMARINE CELEBRITIES

Poseidon was the Greek god of the sea. The brother of Zeus and Hades, he was a very bad-tempered and violent god who caused earthquakes as well as storms. The symbol of his power is a three-pronged spear called a trident.

Hans Christian Andersen wrote *The Little Mermaid*. In this sad story, the mermaid falls in love with a human prince whom she sees when she is allowed to swim to the surface. Her fish tail is changed into legs by the sea witch, and she goes to the shore. The prince takes her to his palace, but he doesn't marry her and she dies.

Gilgamesh was a legendary Mesopotamian king whose exploits are told in a story called *The Epic of Gilgamesh*. One of his many heroic deeds was to dive to the bottom of the sea to find the seaweed that gave eternal life.

Captain Nemo (whose name means "no one") was the hero of Jules Verne's novel, *Twenty Thousand Leagues Under the Sea*. Nemo built a powerful submarine called the *Nautilus* in which he lived and explored the sea.

Augustus Siebe invented the diving dress in 1819. Air was pumped into the helmet through a hose and escaped under the diver's jacket. If the diver fell over the helmet flooded and he could drown. Siebe improved his design a few years later.

John P. Holland was an Irish American who built the first modern practical submarine in 1900. His first idea 25 years before had been for a one-man submarine propelled by cycle pedals.

Lieutenant-Commander von Arnauld of the German navy was the most successful submarine commander in history. During World War I he sank over 150 ships. He was also one of the most gentlemanly of U-boat captains: He always gave the enemy crew time to get to their lifeboats.

Jacques-Yves Cousteau was the co-inventor with Emile Gagnan in 1943 of the Aqua-Lung, which revolutionized diving. Air was carried in cylinders on the diver's back so that for the first time people could swim freely underwater. Cousteau devoted his life to exploration of the underwater world.

Auguste Piccard was a Swiss professor who designed a balloon in the 1930s and flew higher than anyone had ever been. He then decided to explore the depths of the sea. He built a bathyscape or deep-diving vessel, the *Trieste*, which sank 35,800 ft. (10,900 m) into the Marianas Trench in the Pacific Ocean.

LEGENDS OF THE DEEP

Before the technology was developed that allowed us to explore the extreme depths of the ocean, what lay more than a few feet below the surface was a mystery. It is not surprising, then, that there were many tales of strange creatures living beneath the waves.

An ancient legend told of the island of Atlantis that had disappeared under the ocean. According to this myth, the wealthy people of Atlantis became immoral, and earthquakes caused the island to sink.

Most stories were about mermaids, who were half-woman and half-fish. They were said to be beautiful and full of mischief. The dugong, or sea cow, was probably the inspiration behind the legend of the mermaid.

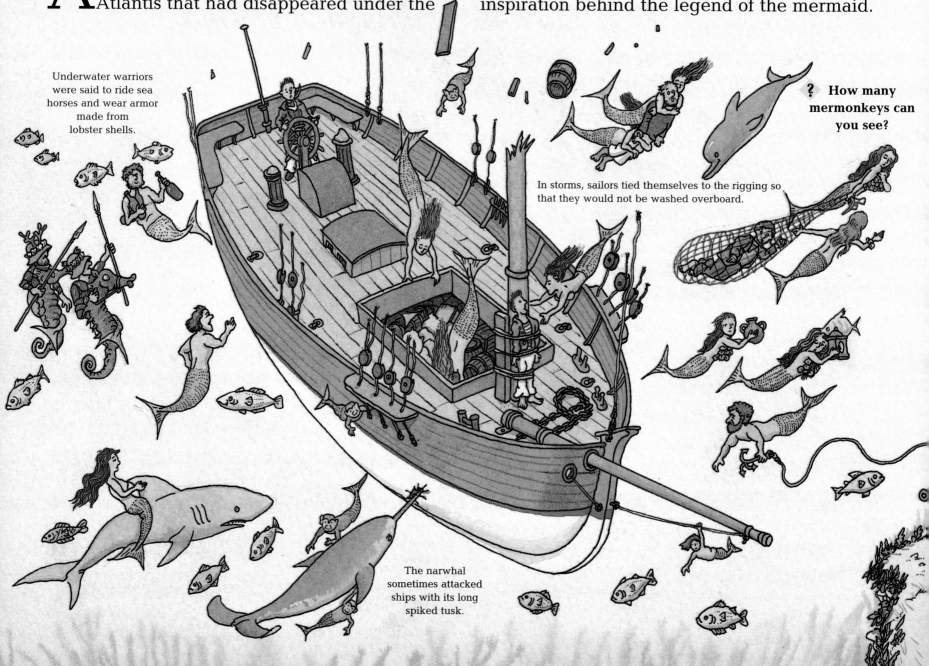

Underwater warriors were said to ride sea horses and wear armor made from lobster shells.

? **How many mermonkeys can you see?**

In storms, sailors tied themselves to the rigging so that they would not be washed overboard.

The narwhal sometimes attacked ships with its long spiked tusk.

There were also sightings of mermen and mermonkeys who, unlike mermaids, were ugly and unfriendly.

The palace of this undersea king and queen is made from parts of wrecked ships.

This is a *dugong*. Dugongs graze on underwater meadows of sea grass.

Monsters of the Deep

The kraken was a huge monster believed to live off the coast of Norway. It lay on the bottom of the sea, warmed by the fires of hell and feeding on giant sea worms. The legend was probably inspired by the sight of a giant squid.

The great sea serpent was reported to have been seen by sailors in the middle of the oceans and was rumored to be responsible for the mysterious disappearance of many ships.

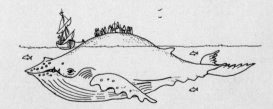

The leviathan was a huge creature mentioned in the Bible and many other sources. It was so vast that tales were told of sailors mistaking it for an island. A Danish bishop was said to have held a religious service on its back.

THE WONDERS OF A CORAL REEF

Coral is very strange. It looks like a plant, feels like rock, but it is really an animal. The hard substance we see is made up of the skeletons of billions of tiny living creatures. These creatures are called polyps, and they feed on tiny algae and chemicals in the sea.

In shallow water, where billions of polyps make a colony, a reef is built up. These reefs form a living mass of beautiful colors. Coral grows into many complex shapes, some of which have odd names, such as brain coral.

Coral reefs are home to a variety of marine life and so are popular with divers. Coral needs sun and warmth so most reefs are found in tropical waters such as off the coast of Australia and in the Caribbean. There are many different kinds of coral: soft coral, hard coral, and even stinging coral. The reef depicted in this drawing is in the Caribbean Sea.

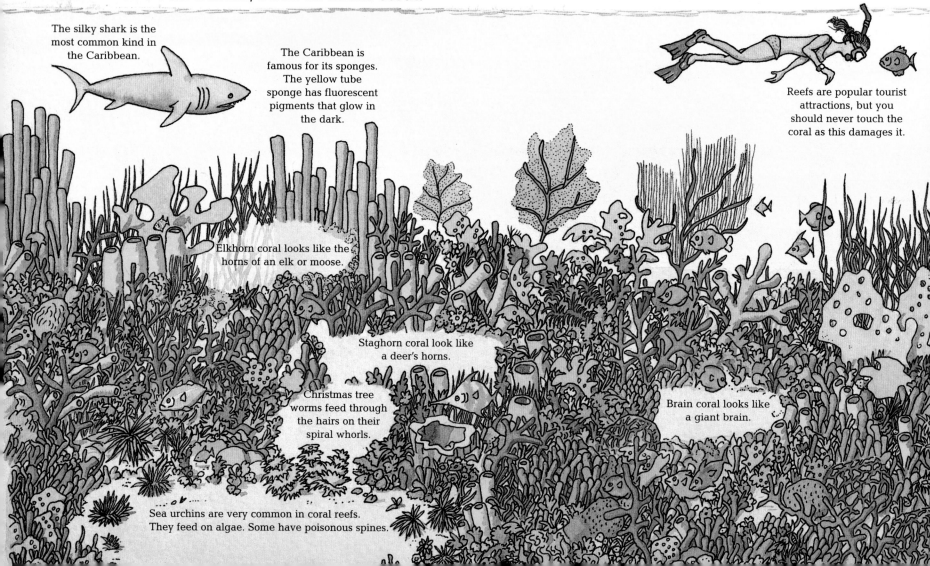

The silky shark is the most common kind in the Caribbean.

The Caribbean is famous for its sponges. The yellow tube sponge has fluorescent pigments that glow in the dark.

Reefs are popular tourist attractions, but you should never touch the coral as this damages it.

Elkhorn coral looks like the horns of an elk or moose.

Staghorn coral look like a deer's horns.

Christmas tree worms feed through the hairs on their spiral whorls.

Brain coral looks like a giant brain.

Sea urchins are very common in coral reefs. They feed on algae. Some have poisonous spines.

Despite their size, reefs are very fragile and can easily be damaged by storms or pollution, which poisons and kills the coral. For these reasons some coral reefs have become endangered.

? **How many blue surgeonfish can you find?**

A blue surgeonfish.

Fan coral grows at right angles to the current to capture more food.

A sea lily feeds through its curling tentacles.

A sea anemone is a solitary polyp.

Coral Creations

The Australian Great Barrier Reef is over 1,250 miles (2,000 km) long. It is about 10,000 years old and is the largest and oldest living thing in the world.

Coral will attach itself to any rock or hard surface. After years spent on the seabed, this crashed airplane has become an oddly shaped coral reef.

Red coral is found on the bottom of the Mediterranean Sea. Divers collect it to be made into necklaces and brooches. It is very rare and expensive.

"THERE SHE BLOWS!"

"There she blows!" was the cry of the lookout on a whaling ship when the waterspout of a whale was spotted. A boat would be launched to chase the whale, with a harpooner standing at the bow. When he was close enough, he threw his harpoon. The whale was not usually killed at once but swam off towing the boat along until the whale was exhausted. When the whale had stopped swimming, it was killed with long lances. The dead whale was then dragged back to the ship and cut up. Its blubber or fat was boiled down to make whale oil, and its meat was dried to be eaten.

Whales are not fish: they are mammals and must come to the surface to breathe.

The sperm whale is the largest of the toothed whales. It can grow to an incredible 65 ft. (20 m) in length and weigh 50 tons. It feeds on giant squid that it catches at depths of 1,640 ft. (500 m) or more.

A giant squid can measure up to 65 ft. (20 m) in length, including its tentacles.

Whales have been hunted for over a thousand years, but today's hunting methods are so efficient that many species of whale are almost extinct. Many countries have now agreed to stop hunting the whale until its numbers increase.

The blowhole is where a whale breathes out, causing the famous spout.

? **How many dolphins can you see?**

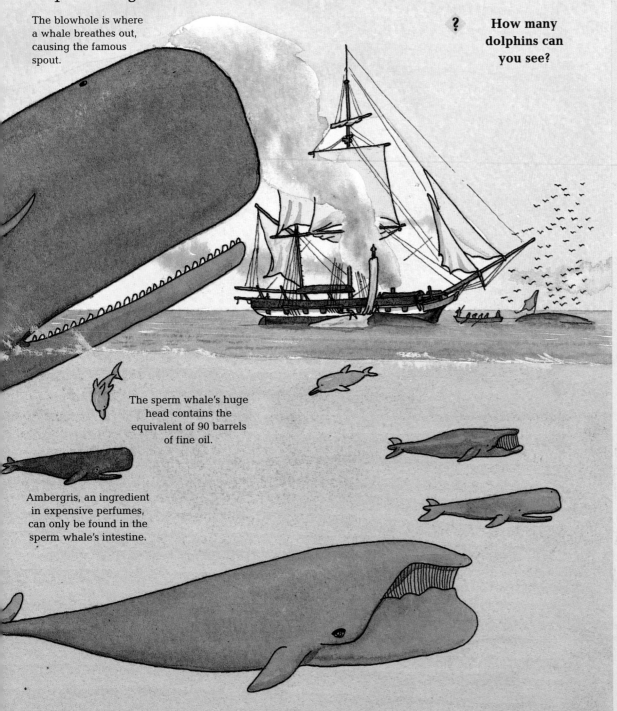

The sperm whale's huge head contains the equivalent of 90 barrels of fine oil.

Ambergris, an ingredient in expensive perfumes, can only be found in the sperm whale's intestine.

Whale Wonders

Baleen or "whalebone" was once used to make stays or corsets. The Victorian fashion for tiny waists almost caused the extinction of the Greenland whale.

Before electricity, much of the world's artificial light came from whale oil, which is obtained from blubber. Whale oil was also used to make soap, varnish, and to lubricate machinery.

Scrimshaw is the name given to the art of carving patterns on shells, whales' teeth, and walrus' tusks. American seamen developed scrimshaw in the early 1800s. Supposedly it takes its name from one Admiral Scrimshaw, an expert carver.

UNDERWATER TREASURE HUNT

Thousands of ships lie forgotten at the bottom of the sea. From ancient Greek galleys to Atlantic liners, they all rot and rust beneath the waves. However, it is surprising what survives, even after 2,000 years underwater.

In the past, divers were interested in wrecks only for their monetarily valuable cargoes but, since the 1950s, underwater archaeologists have examined wrecks in a scientific way. Archaeologists can tell us how ships were built in the past and, by recovering ordinary objects,

they can learn how sailors lived and worked. A ship's cargo tells us what trade went on between countries. For example, many ancient Greek wrecks contain jars that once held olive oil. Wrecks are full of interesting things besides gold.

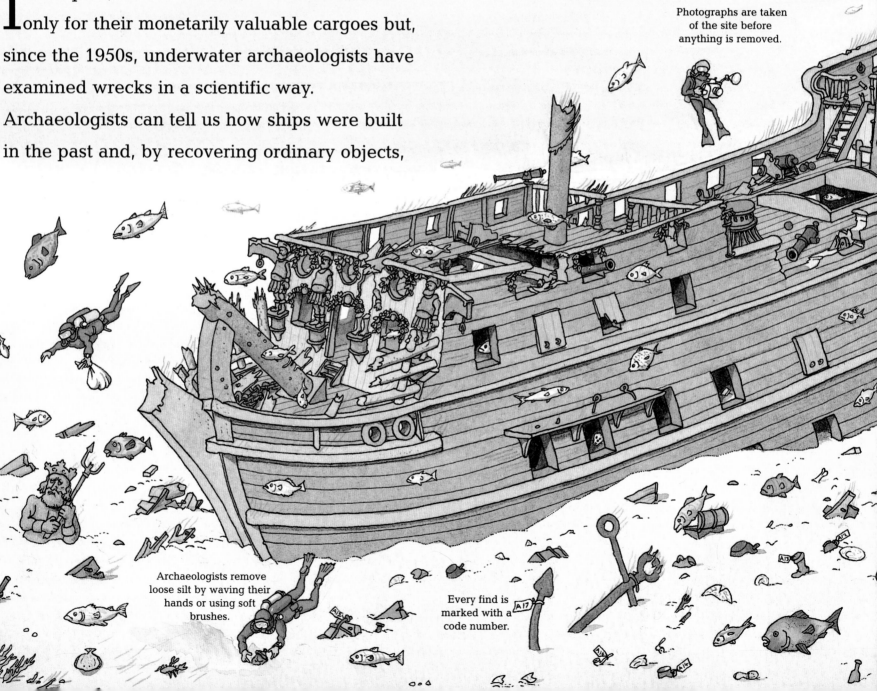

Photographs are taken of the site before anything is removed.

Archaeologists remove loose silt by waving their hands or using soft brushes.

Every find is marked with a code number.

A grid of poles is laid out on the wreck so the exact positions of objects can be plotted.

This diver is using an airlift to suck up mud.

Air-filled bags are used to lift heavy objects. Divers tie the empty bags to the things they find on the seabed, then fill the bags with air.

This diver is using a water jet to blow away mud.

? How many cannons can you find in this picture?

Divers draw everything they find with crayons on plastic sheets.

Remarkable Wrecks

The oldest wrecked ship ever found was discovered off the coast of Turkey at Ulburun in 1984. It sank in about 1316 B.C.—over 3,000 years ago—and was carrying a cargo of copper, tin, glass, gold trinkets, and jars of perfume.

In 1628 the warship *Vasa*, the pride of Sweden, sank in Stockholm harbor. She lay on the bottom perfectly preserved until she was rediscovered and raised to the surface in 1961.

The *Titanic* is the most famous shipwreck of all. The great liner hit an iceberg on her first voyage and sank in 13,000 ft. (4,000 m) of water. It would have taken her almost two hours to reach the bottom.

WAR UNDERWATER

Making war underwater was a military ambition for hundreds of years. How empowering it would be to have a ship that hid beneath the sea and sank its enemies in perfect safety! Many inventors thought about submarines and some built them, but they all sank or were too slow to attack ships.

During the American Civil War, the Confederate force had submarines that they hoped would give them an advantage over the much more powerful Union fleet.

The first submarine to sink a ship was the *H. L. Hunley*. One night in 1864 it sailed up to the USS *Housatonic*, which was anchored off the port of Charleston, and torpedoed her. The *Housatonic* sank in a few minutes, but a wave from the explosion entered the open hatch of the *H. L. Hunley* and swamped the craft. The entire crew was drowned.

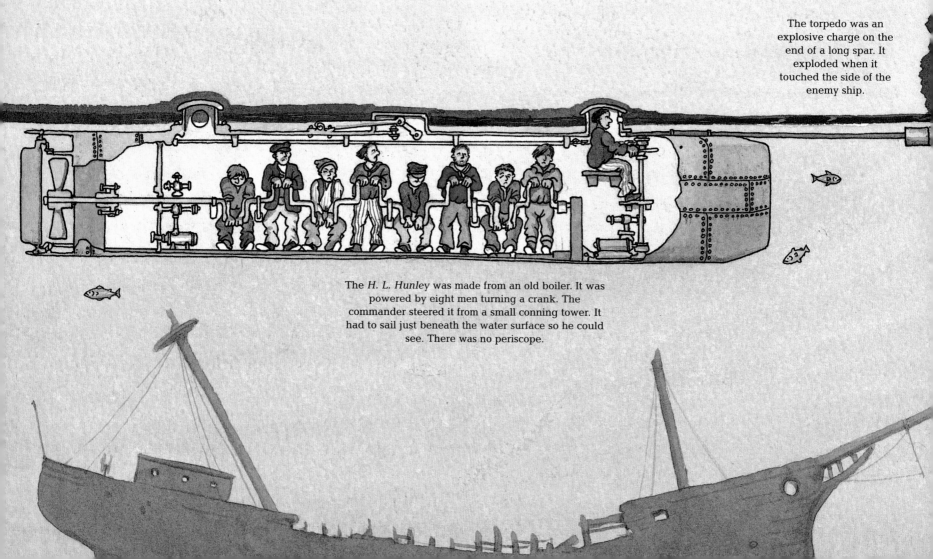

The torpedo was an explosive charge on the end of a long spar. It exploded when it touched the side of the enemy ship.

The *H. L. Hunley* was made from an old boiler. It was powered by eight men turning a crank. The commander steered it from a small conning tower. It had to sail just beneath the water surface so he could see. There was no periscope.

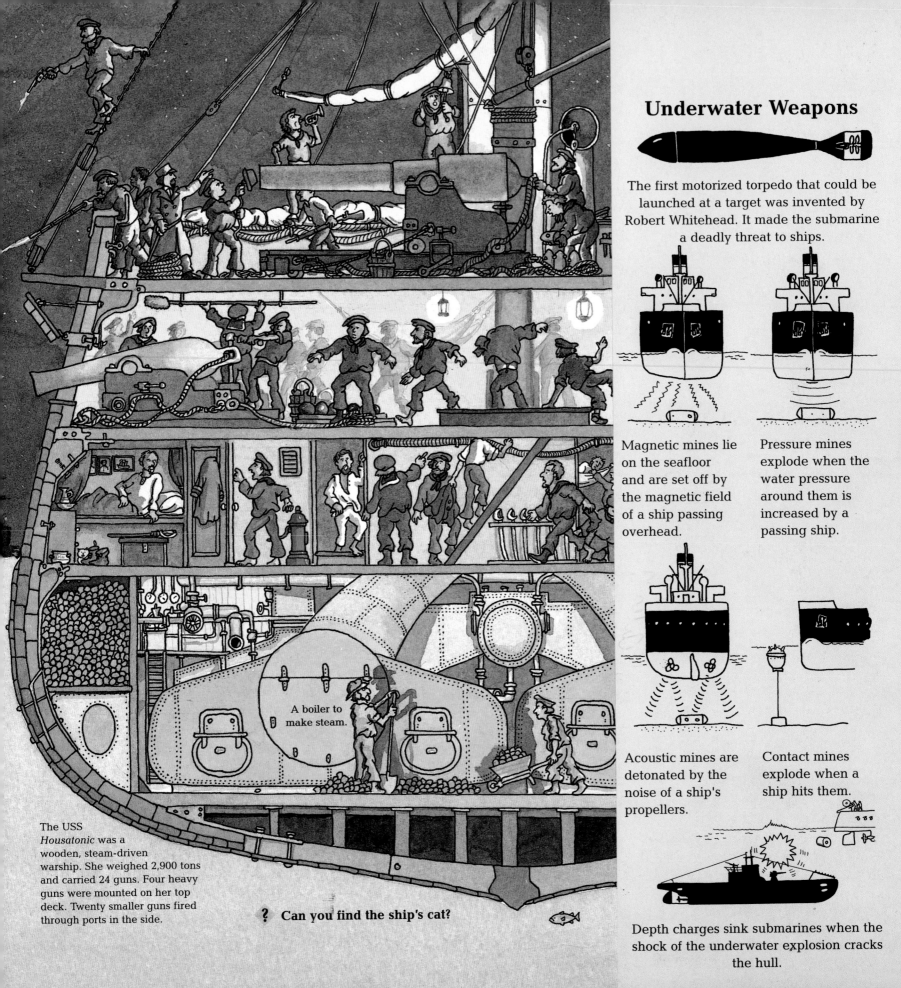

The USS *Housatonic* was a wooden, steam-driven warship. She weighed 2,900 tons and carried 24 guns. Four heavy guns were mounted on her top deck. Twenty smaller guns fired through ports in the side.

A boiler to make steam.

? Can you find the ship's cat?

Underwater Weapons

The first motorized torpedo that could be launched at a target was invented by Robert Whitehead. It made the submarine a deadly threat to ships.

Magnetic mines lie on the seafloor and are set off by the magnetic field of a ship passing overhead.

Pressure mines explode when the water pressure around them is increased by a passing ship.

Acoustic mines are detonated by the noise of a ship's propellers.

Contact mines explode when a ship hits them.

Depth charges sink submarines when the shock of the underwater explosion cracks the hull.

DIVING DEEP

For thousands of years people used the technique of "free diving," which meant that they could only stay underwater for as long as they could hold their breath. Inventors tried to develop ways in which divers could breathe underwater, but none really worked until Augustus Siebe, a German inventor, created the first practical diving suit in 1819. Air was forced down a pipe into the diver's helmet by a pump aboard a ship and escaped through a gap at the diver's waist. This was fine so long as the diver stayed upright. Siebe modified the suit to make it airtight, and with the new design divers could descend to 65 ft. (20 m).

Divers could suddenly do all sorts of work on the seabed, such as building foundations for bridges and docks, clearing wrecks and other obstructions, and salvaging treasure from sunken ships.

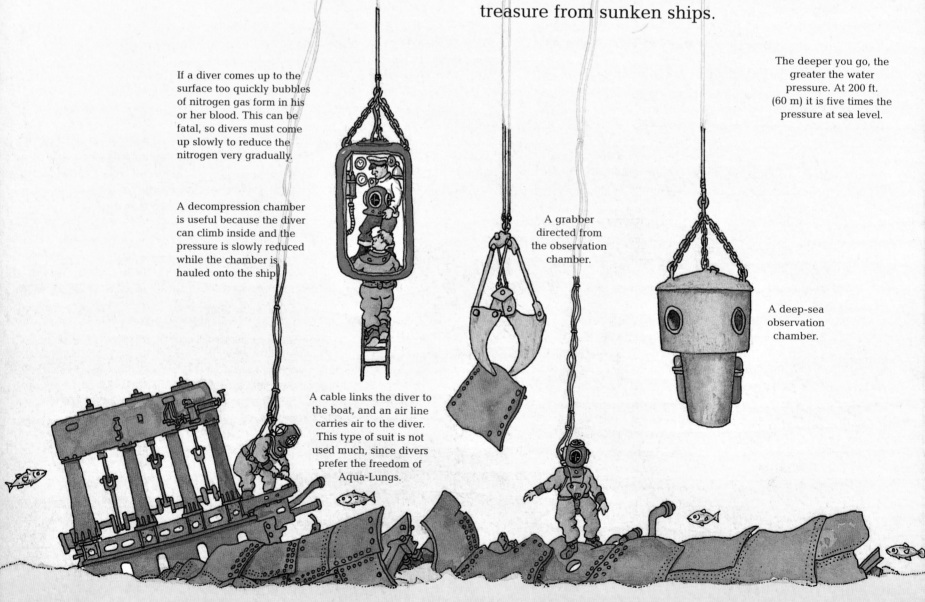

If a diver comes up to the surface too quickly bubbles of nitrogen gas form in his or her blood. This can be fatal, so divers must come up slowly to reduce the nitrogen very gradually.

A decompression chamber is useful because the diver can climb inside and the pressure is slowly reduced while the chamber is hauled onto the ship.

A cable links the diver to the boat, and an air line carries air to the diver. This type of suit is not used much, since divers prefer the freedom of Aqua-Lungs.

A grabber directed from the observation chamber.

The deeper you go, the greater the water pressure. At 200 ft. (60 m) it is five times the pressure at sea level.

A deep-sea observation chamber.

? How many fish can you find in the ship?

In 1888 English diver Alexander Lambert salvaged $129,545 of Spanish gold from the *Alphonso XII* sunk off the Canary Islands. The ship was lying in water 170 ft. (52 m) deep. Lambert had to blast his way through three decks to get to the strong room, and to descend nine times to get all the gold.

Daring Divers

In 450 B.C. two Greek divers, Scyllias and his daughter Cyana, cut the anchor ropes of Persian warships that were invading Greece. A storm arose and drove the ships onto rocks where they sank.

Japanese ama women do all the diving in their communities. They used to dive for pearls but now dive for shellfish and edible seaweed. They stay below for a minute and can reach a depth of 100 ft. (30 m).

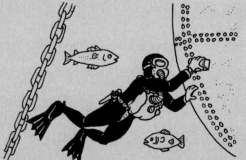

During World War II, frogmen used Self-Contained Underwater Breathing Apparatus—or SCUBA diving equipment —to swim into enemy ports on secret sabotage missions.

WORKING UNDERWATER

There is always work to be done underwater: building foundations for bridges and docks, clearing harbors of sand and mud, and removing wrecks. It was almost impossible to do any of this until the invention of the diving bell and the dredger.

The first diving bell was invented by an Italian called Gugliemo de Lorena in the 16th century. Air pumped down under pressure kept water out of the bell, which remained dry. It allowed a person to work underwater without wearing a suit, and it was very useful for laying stones on the seabed or working on wrecks.

Ships called dredgers are used to scoop up sand and mud from the seabed.

A suction dredger.

Hoisting tackle.

Mud pours into the hopper barge from the nozzle.

The centrifugal pump sucks up mud.

? **Supermarket carts are everywhere. How many can you find?**

Mud and sand are sucked up through this pipe.

All types of poisonous material are dumped at sea. People used to think it did not matter, but now we understand the damage pollution does to marine life.

This remote-controlled machine can perform tasks using the arms of the vessel.

Rotating nozzle.

The most common form of dredger is fitted with an endless chain of buckets that drag or "dredge" along the seabed, then tip their contents into a barge tied alongside.

When the seabed is made up of silt or soft mud, a suction dredger can be used. This sucks up everything through a pipe like a gigantic vacuum cleaner.

Underwater Tools

It seems odd to think that heat can be generated underwater, but engineers use welding and cutting equipment underwater just as easily as on land.

The underwater version of the pneumatic drill is very useful for drilling holes in rock for placing explosives.

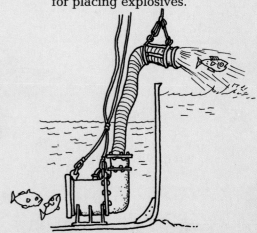

Underwater pumps are powered by electric motors that actually work in water. Pumps are often used to pump water out of sunken ships that can then be raised to the surface.

Lifting tackle.

Air lock.

Machinery for raising and lowering the diving bell.

Engine room.

Air shaft.

Divers drill holes in the rock. They then put explosives in the holes and blow the rock into tiny pieces so that it can be cleared away.

Hydraulic cement sets underwater.

A Tunnel Beneath the Sea

Although the channel between England and France is only 18 miles (30 km) wide, the sea is often rough and crossings can be dangerous. The first practical idea for a tunnel came from a French engineer, Albert Mathieu, but it was technically impossible to achieve at the time. In 1880, digging began on both sides of the channel but was halted after a year. The British army was against the tunnel—some generals thought the French might creep through to invade England!

The project was forgotten until 1973, then restarted only to be abandoned again when it proved too expensive.

Huge crossover caves were built where the two rail tunnels merge into one. The caves are the size of small cathedrals: 550 ft. (170 m) long, 70 ft. (21 m) wide and 50 ft. (15.4 m) high.

This cave lies below about 230 ft. (70 m) of chalk and 160 ft. (50 m) of seawater.

The movable cutting arm of a machine called a roadheader shapes the soft rock.

At first, the cave is lined with a rough layer of concrete. A smooth layer is added later.

The final attempt to dig a channel tunnel began in 1987 and was finished in 1993. It runs through firm chalk, so there is no danger that the roof will collapse or water will break in.

Today, passengers travel through the tunnel on high-speed trains, and cars and trucks are carried by special shuttles.

? It is very hot in the tunnel, so the engineers need lots of water to drink. How many thermos bottles can you find?

Ventilation duct. Fresh air is pumped 10 miles (17 km) along the tunnel from the surface.

Caves are dug by the roadheaders. When the caves are big enough, huge Tunnel-Boring Machines (TBMs) are brought in to complete the tunnel.

A roadheader.

Submarine Bores

The cutting arms of the rotary Tunnel-Boring Machine (TBM) spin into the rock and break it up. The machine is pushed forward by hydraulic rams, and the tunnel is lined with concrete.

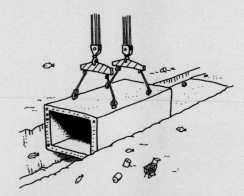

Boring is not the only way to build a tunnel underwater. Where the water is shallow, a trench can be dug, and sections of the tunnel lowered into it. These are joined up, made watertight, then buried.

The Seikan Tunnel in Japan is 33 miles (54 km) long. It took nearly 20 years to build because the underlying rock was very difficult to work with. It was hard and full of cracks and faults.

SEA HARVEST

For centuries, fishermen have braved dangerous seas in search of the best catch. A thousand years ago, Viking fishermen sailed across the Atlantic to distant Newfoundland in search of fish. Today fishing is a multimillion dollar industry, and some fishing vessels can stay at sea for months. Almost every species of fish is taken. Some of this fish is eaten by people, but most of it is turned into animal feed or fertilizer and used on crops. Overfishing is a problem and some species of fish, like herring in the North Sea, are now rare. In 1999 over 100 million tons of fish were caught in the world's oceans.

? How many different kinds of fish can you see?

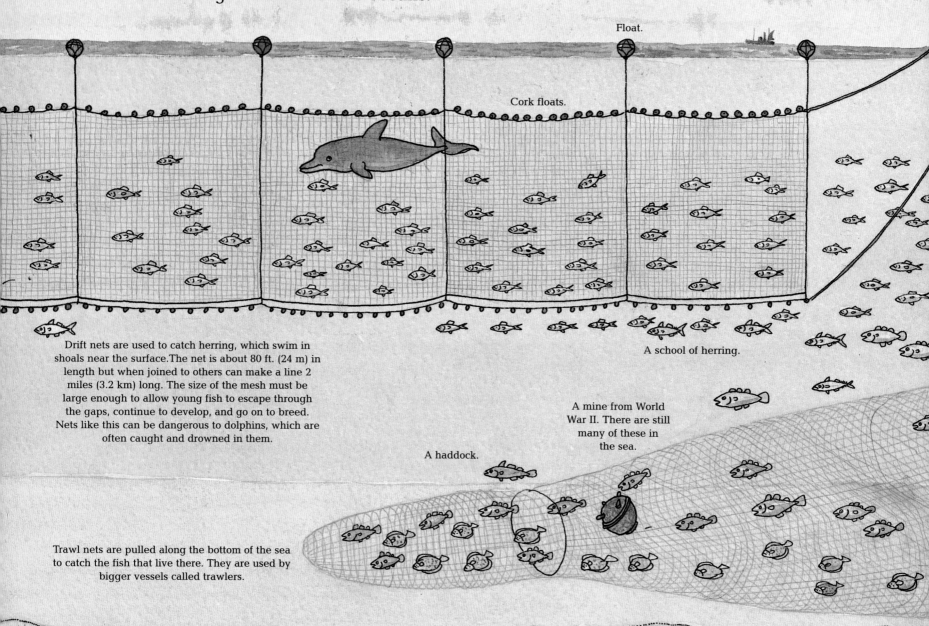

Float.

Cork floats.

Drift nets are used to catch herring, which swim in shoals near the surface. The net is about 80 ft. (24 m) in length but when joined to others can make a line 2 miles (3.2 km) long. The size of the mesh must be large enough to allow young fish to escape through the gaps, continue to develop, and go on to breed. Nets like this can be dangerous to dolphins, which are often caught and drowned in them.

A school of herring.

A mine from World War II. There are still many of these in the sea.

A haddock.

Trawl nets are pulled along the bottom of the sea to catch the fish that live there. They are used by bigger vessels called trawlers.

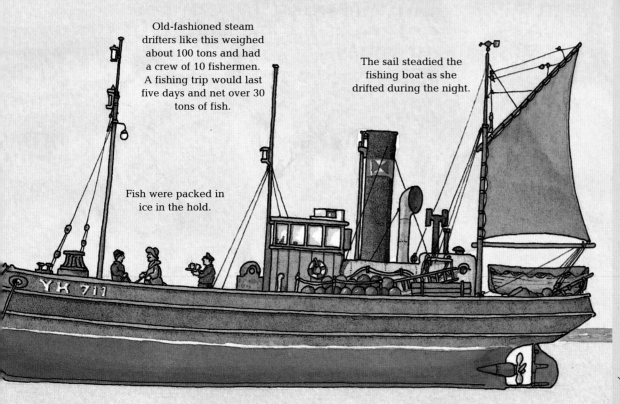

Old-fashioned steam drifters like this weighed about 100 tons and had a crew of 10 fishermen. A fishing trip would last five days and net over 30 tons of fish.

The sail steadied the fishing boat as she drifted during the night.

Fish were packed in ice in the hold.

YK 711

Ways of Fishing

Fishermen in Japan and China use cormorants to catch fish. The birds have a ring round their necks that prevents them from swallowing the fish they bring back to the boats.

Otter boards keep the net open.

When the net is closed and pulled to the surface, it may contain up to 100 tons of fish.

Floats are used to buoy up the top of the net.

Cod and plaice swim into the net.

In Sri Lanka, fishermen perch on long poles in the surf to cast their lines out into the sea.

Crabs and lobsters are caught in these basket traps or "pots." A piece of bait is placed inside the basket, the crab crawls in, down a narrowing funnel, and then can't escape.

DEEP-SEA DETERRENTS

For 40 years the USA and the former Soviet Union (the USSR) threatened each other with nuclear weapons. They both had the problem of keeping their rockets safe from being destroyed by a sudden attack. Nuclear bombs are so dangerous that it's not safe to store them on land. The United States was the first to send its missiles to sea in submarines, where they would cruise hidden in the depths. The USSR followed, and now Great Britain, France, and China have missile submarines.

Nuclear-powered submarines never need to surface to recharge their batteries and can travel for 155,250 miles (250,000 km)

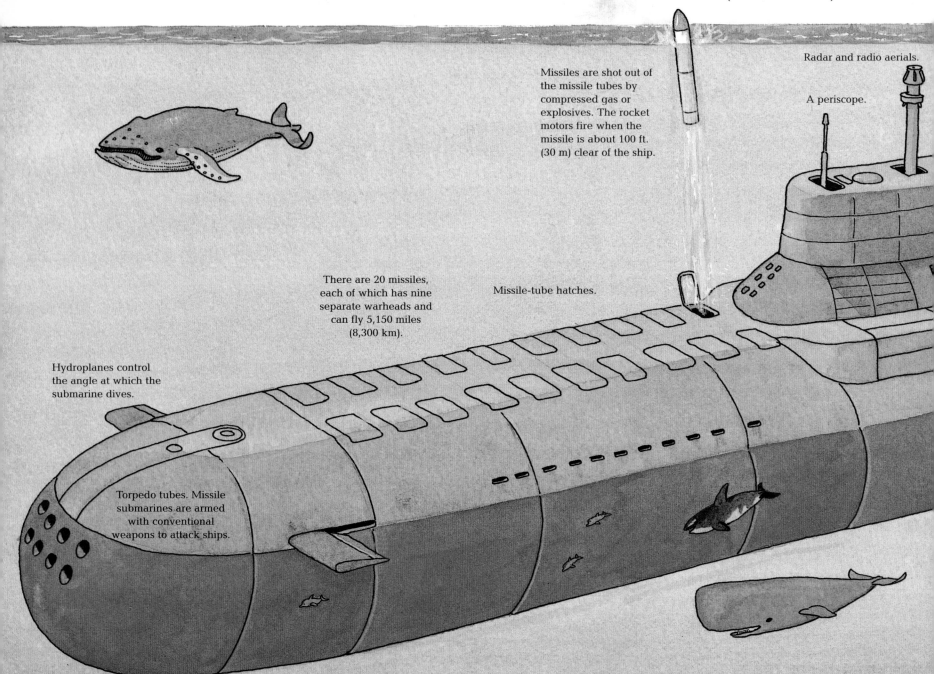

Missiles are shot out of the missile tubes by compressed gas or explosives. The rocket motors fire when the missile is about 100 ft. (30 m) clear of the ship.

Radar and radio aerials.

A periscope.

There are 20 missiles, each of which has nine separate warheads and can fly 5,150 miles (8,300 km).

Missile-tube hatches.

Hydroplanes control the angle at which the submarine dives.

Torpedo tubes. Missile submarines are armed with conventional weapons to attack ships.

without refueling.These submarines carry up to 24 missiles and can hit their targets from any ocean in the world. They spend months at sea, never surfacing and never sending radio messages. The greatest problem the crews suffer is isolation and boredom.

A Century of Submarines

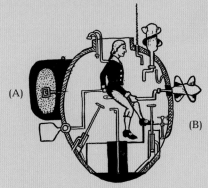

In 1776, during the American War of Independence, Sergeant Ezra Lee made history's first submarine attack in the *Turtle*. He tried to sink HMS *Eagle* in New York harbor by attaching a mine filled with gunpowder (A) to the warship's bottom. The *Turtle* was driven by a hand-cranked propeller (B).

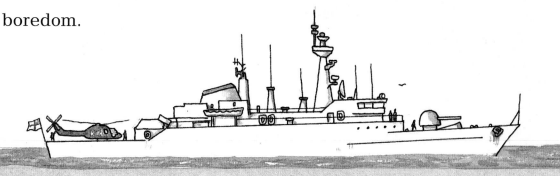

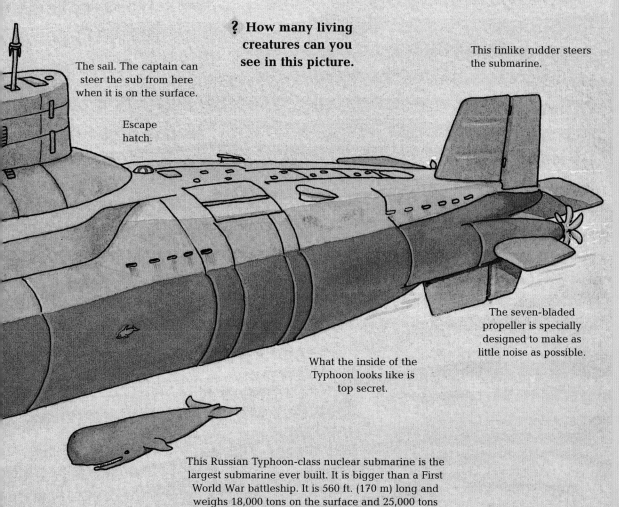

? How many living creatures can you see in this picture.

The sail. The captain can steer the sub from here when it is on the surface.

Escape hatch.

This finlike rudder steers the submarine.

The seven-bladed propeller is specially designed to make as little noise as possible.

What the inside of the Typhoon looks like is top secret.

This Russian Typhoon-class nuclear submarine is the largest submarine ever built. It is bigger than a First World War battleship. It is 560 ft. (170 m) long and weighs 18,000 tons on the surface and 25,000 tons submerged. It has a top underwater speed of 25 knots (30 miles/46km) and can probably dive to about 1,000 ft. (300 m). There is a crew of 150 submariners.

French engineer Monsieur Goubet built this electric submarine in 1886 for the Russian Navy. Like the *Turtle* it was meant to stick an explosive charge (A) to the bottom of an enemy ship.

The American inventor Simon Lake designed this submarine, the *Argonaut Junior,* in 1893. It had wheels so it could run along the seabed and an airlock to allow the driver to get in and out while underwater.

SUBMARINE LABORATORY

Although people might dream of living underwater and of building cities on the ocean floor, it would be incredibly expensive and difficult to achieve. Most likely, the only people who would live for periods underwater in the future would be engineers working on pipelines, miners controlling remote machines, fish farmers, or research scientists.

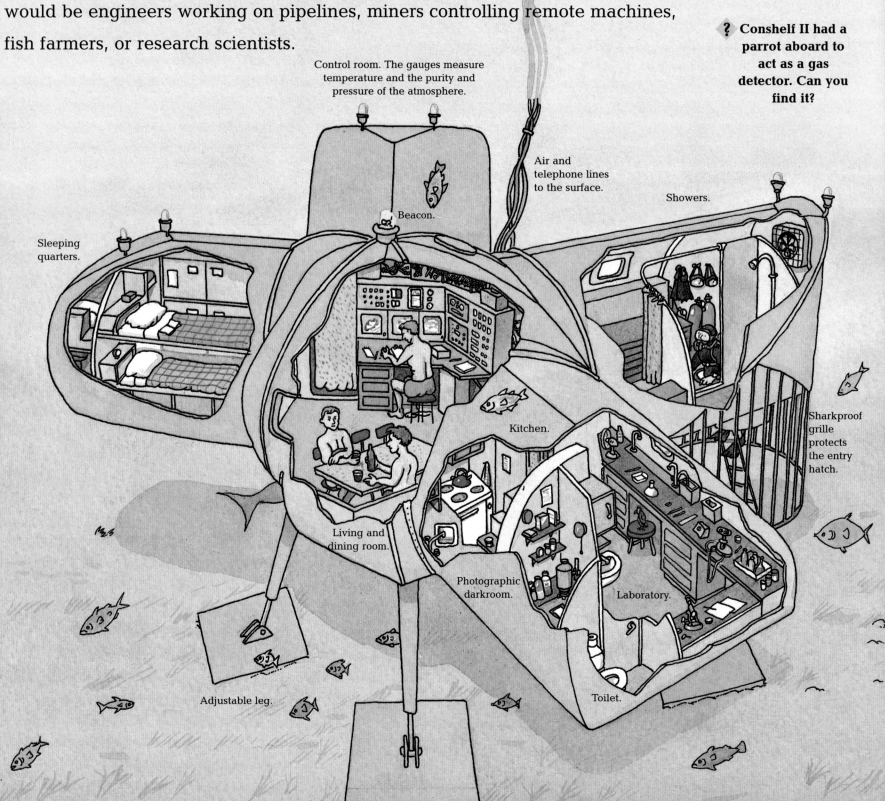

? Conshelf II had a parrot aboard to act as a gas detector. Can you find it?

Control room. The gauges measure temperature and the purity and pressure of the atmosphere.

Air and telephone lines to the surface.

Showers.

Beacon.

Sleeping quarters.

Kitchen.

Sharkproof grille protects the entry hatch.

Living and dining room.

Photographic darkroom.

Laboratory.

Adjustable leg.

Toilet.

Jacques-Yves Cousteau, the famous French explorer and oceanographer, designed an experimental colony to test the ability of people to live and work underwater. Conshelf II was sunk 32 ft. (10 m) underwater in the Red Sea. Five men lived there for a month, going out every day to explore and do experiments. Although they were living under pressure, they stayed healthy and didn't get on each other's nerves. Two odd effects of the pressure were that beards grew more slowly, but cuts healed faster.

Dwellings in the Deep

Conshelf III was Cousteau's next experiment. It was sunk 330 ft. (100 m) in the Mediterranean. The living quarters were in a sphere designed to resist the underwater pressure. The crew breathed an atmosphere made of 98 percent helium and 2 percent oxygen, which made them all sound like Donald Duck.

Hydrolab was an American underwater laboratory in the Bahamas. It operated from 1972 to 1985, and hundreds of scientists used it.

When they are working on the seafloor, divers live in pressurized cabins so they don't waste time surfacing when they need a break.

Garage for diving saucer.

The diving saucer can dive to 3,000 ft. (900 m). It is powered by jets of seawater and is steered by moving the nozzles of the jets.

Pump.

Fiberglass outer casing.

Steel inner shell.

Batteries.

Toolshed.

Claw.

UNDERWATER GEAR

A design for a diving suit from the 16th century. It would never have worked because the differences in water pressure would not have allowed the diver to draw air from the surface.

Augustus Siebe perfected the first fully enclosed diving suit in 1837. Air was pumped down into the helmet, and the diver wore lead boots and weights to keep him on the seabed. The design remained in use for over a hundred years.

Two Frenchmen, the Carmagnole brothers, built this weird-looking diving armor in 1882. It had 20 windows and 22 joints.

William James made the first self-contained diving dress in 1825. The air was stored in an iron cylinder worn around the waist.

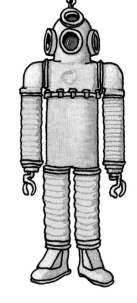

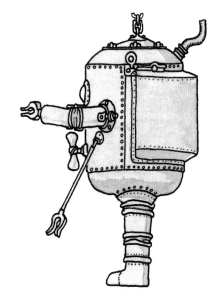

This suit was designed in 1920 to operate at a depth of 328 ft. (100 m). However, water pressure would have collapsed the flexible arms and legs.

Giovanni Borelli designed this suit with webbed feet in 1680 so that "man could swim like a frog." It didn't work.

This armored suit with joints was designed by L.D. Phillips in 1865. It enabled divers to move more easily and breathe air at normal pressure.

This strange suit, made in 1930, was the first diving armor to be really successful. Flexible joints allowed the diver to work at depths of 990 ft. (300 m).

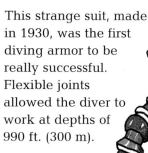

The modern diving suit, called a NEWT suit, has much more fluid joints and an electric thruster to help the diver move about.

Frogmen in World War II used oxygen "rebreathers." Chemicals in the unit removed poisonous carbon dioxide from the exhaled air so that the diver could breathe it in again. This meant that there were no telltale bubbles to give away the diver's position, but the frogman could not dive below 26 ft. (8 m).

This modern underwater vessel can dive to 2,000 ft. (600 m). Its transparent bubble is made of very strong plastic and provides wonderful all-round views. It can stay underwater for ten hours.

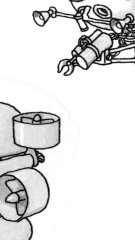

Diving bells, where the pressure of the air trapped inside keeps out the water, have been around since the Middle Ages, but the first really useful one was developed by Sir Edmond Halley —the astronomer after whom the comet is named. Barrels full of air were sent down from the surface.

Deep-diving machines like this are used for exploration, salvage, and working on oil equipment on the seabed. This one can dive to 985 ft. (300 m).

Glossary

Atlantis: This mythical island in the Atlantic Ocean was said to have been swallowed up by a huge wave caused by an earthquake.

Baleen: Baleen is also known as "whalebone," but it is not bone at all. It is a hornlike material that hangs down from the top of a toothless whale's jaw. The whale uses it to strain the plankton it eats from the seawater.

Caribbean Sea: This sea is actually part of the Atlantic Ocean. It is surrounded by the West Indies, Central America, and the northern coast of South America.

Dugong: Dugongs are known as sea cows because they graze on underwater meadows of sea grass. They live in the Red Sea and the Indian and Pacific Oceans.

Galleon: A galleon is a large sailing ship with three or more masts.

Narwhal: A narwhal is a kind of whale that lives in the Arctic Ocean. Male narwhals have a long spiral tusk.

Torpedo: A torpedo is a long tube filled with explosives. Torpedoes can be launched from airplanes, ships, or submarines.

Answers

pages 10–11 There are 5 mermonkeys.

pages 12–13 There are 8 blue surgeonfish.

pages 14–15 There are 4 dolphins.

pages 16–17 There are 9 cannons.

pages 18–19 The ship's cat is hiding under a bed.

pages 20–21 There are 12 fish in the ship.

pages 22–23 There are 7 supermarket carts.

pages 24–25 There are 6 thermos bottles.

pages 26-27 There are 5 different species: mackerel, herring, haddock, plaice, and cod.

pages 28–29 The answer is 16: 4 whales, 4 dolphins, 5 people, and 3 seagulls.

pages 30–31 The parrot is in the laboratory.